D1378915

STATE PROFILES
CALIFORNIA

BY EMILY ROSE OACHS

BELLWETHER MEDIA • MINNEAPOLIS, MN

Blastoff! Discovery launches a new mission: reading to learn. Filled with facts and features, each book offers you an exciting new world to explore!

BLASTOFF! UNIVERSE

BLASTOFF! Beginners — GRADE K

BLASTOFF! READERS — GRADES 1-3

BLASTOFF! DISCOVERY — GRADE 4

This edition first published in 2022 by Bellwether Media, Inc.

No part of this publication may be reproduced in whole or in part without written permission of the publisher.
For information regarding permission, write to Bellwether Media, Inc., Attention: Permissions Department,
6012 Blue Circle Drive, Minnetonka, MN 55343.

Library of Congress Cataloging-in-Publication Data

Names: Oachs, Emily Rose, author.
Title: California / by Emily Rose Oachs.
Description: Minneapolis, MN : Bellwether Media, Inc., 2022. |
    Series: Blastoff! Discovery: State profiles | Includes bibliographical
    references and index. | Audience: Ages 7-13 | Audience: Grades
    4-6 | Summary: "Engaging images accompany information about
    California. The combination of high-interest subject matter and
    narrative text is intended for students in grades 3 through 8"–
    Provided by publisher.
Identifiers: LCCN 2021019639 (print) | LCCN 2021019640 (ebook)
    | ISBN 9781644873762 (library binding) | ISBN
    9781648341533 (ebook)
Subjects: LCSH: California–Juvenile literature.
Classification: LCC F861.3 .O23 2022 (print) | LCC F861.3 (ebook)
    | DDC 979.4–dc23
LC record available at https://lccn.loc.gov/2021019639
LC ebook record available at https://lccn.loc.gov/2021019640

Editor: Colleen Sexton   Designer: Brittany McIntosh

Printed in the United States of America, North Mankato, MN.

TABLE OF CONTENTS

Griffith Park	4
Where Is California?	6
California's Beginnings	8
Landscape and Climate	10
Wildlife	12
People and Communities	14
San Diego	16
Industry	18
Food	20
Sports and Entertainment	22
Festivals and Traditions	24
California Timeline	26
California Facts	28
Glossary	30
To Learn More	31
Index	32

GRIFFITH PARK

    In Griffith Park, a family climbs a winding path up a dusty
mountain trail. The sun shines brightly overhead. Soon,
the trail widens. The beautiful Griffith **Observatory** lies
ahead. Behind it stands the city of Los Angeles. Streets and
buildings stretch in all directions. In the distance, the family
spots the blue water of the Pacific Ocean.

GRIFFITH OBSERVATORY

DISNEYLAND

GOLDEN GATE BRIDGE

JOSHUA TREE NATIONAL PARK

YOSEMITE NATIONAL PARK

A SIGN OF THE TIMES

The Hollywood sign was built in 1923 to advertise a nearby neighborhood. Until 1949, it read *Hollywoodland*. Each letter stands 45 feet (14 meters) tall!

On a far-off mountain, the family catches a glimpse of the famed Hollywood sign. Its white letters stand out against the brown and green mountainside. Rugged hills, sparkling Pacific waters, and booming industry all help make this state great. Welcome to California!

N
W ✛ E
S

California is in the western
United States. This long and narrow
state covers 163,695 square miles
(423,968 square kilometers).
It is the country's third-largest state.
California's western border touches
the Pacific Ocean. Oregon lies to the
north. California shares its eastern
border with Nevada and Arizona.
Mexico meets the southern border.

The capital city of Sacramento sits in
northern California. The state's largest
cities lie on the coast. San Francisco
is in the north. Los Angeles and
San Diego are in the south. The state's
major rivers include the Sacramento
and the Colorado.

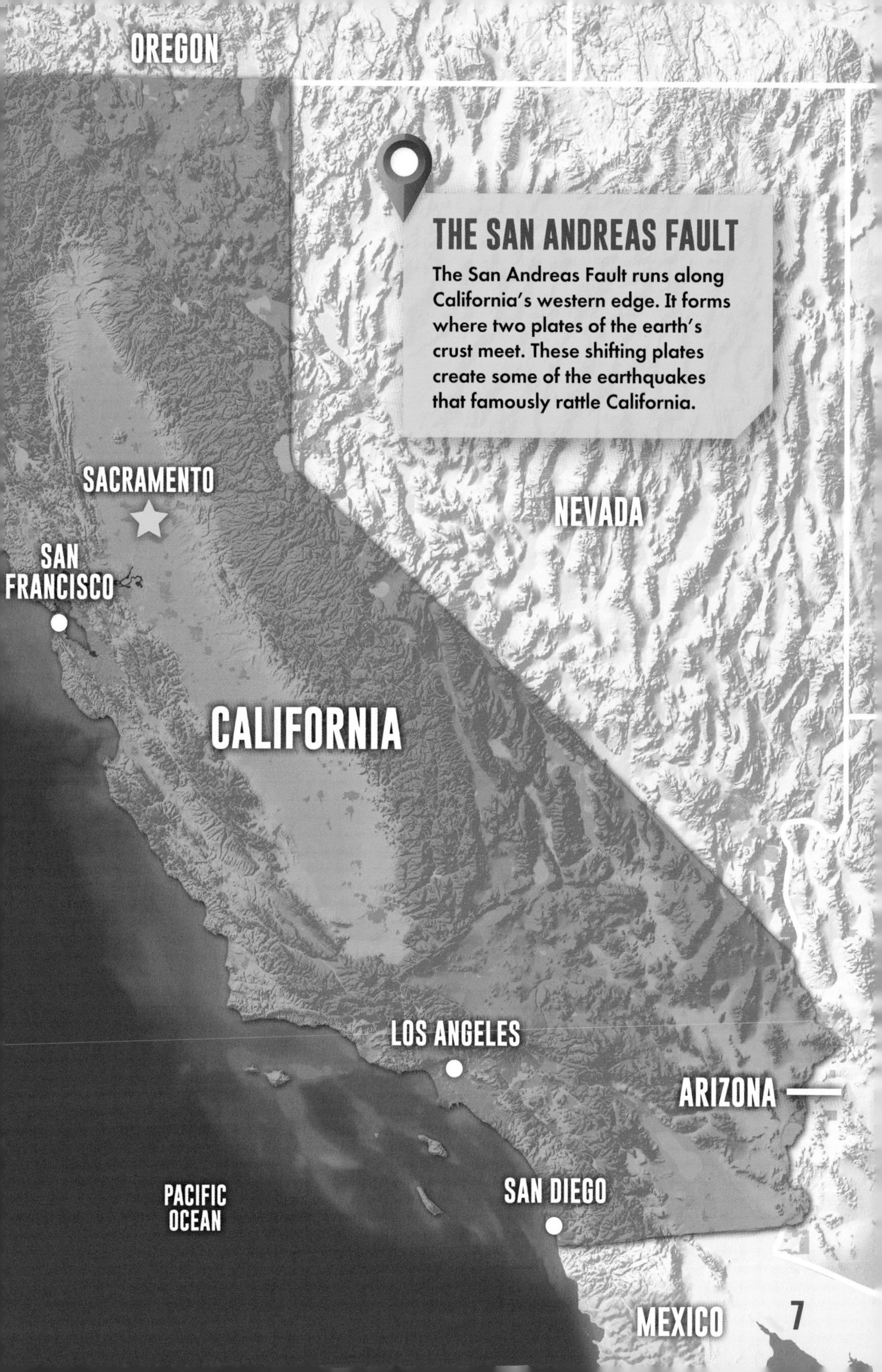

OREGON

THE SAN ANDREAS FAULT

The San Andreas Fault runs along California's western edge. It forms where two plates of the earth's crust meet. These shifting plates create some of the earthquakes that famously rattle California.

SACRAMENTO

NEVADA

SAN FRANCISCO

CALIFORNIA

LOS ANGELES

ARIZONA

SAN DIEGO

PACIFIC OCEAN

MEXICO

CALIFORNIA MISSIONS

Between 1769 and 1823, Spanish priests founded 21 missions in California. They dotted the western coast from San Diego to San Francisco. Each mission was about one day's walk to the next.

The first Californians arrived over 10,000 years ago. In time, they formed dozens of Native American tribes. They included the Yurok, Chumash, and Pomo. In 1542, Spanish explorers reached California. Spanish priests arrived about 200 years later. They set up **missions** to **convert** Native Americans to Christianity. Many Native Americans were also forced to give up their **traditional** ways and perform labor.

Mexico won control of California in 1821 and soon broke up the missions. In 1848, gold discovered at Sutter's Mill drew thousands of gold seekers. That same year, the United States gained control of California. In 1850, California became the 31st state.

NATIVE PEOPLES OF CALIFORNIA

YUROK PEOPLE

- Original lands in northern California around the Klamath River
- About 5,000 live in California today
- Also called Pohlik-la, Ner-er-er, Petch-ik-lah, and Klamath River Indians

CHUMASH PEOPLE

- Original lands on the Channel Islands and in coastal southern California
- About 5,000 live in California today

POMO PEOPLE

- Original lands along the coast of northern California
- About 4,500 live in California today

Towering redwood forests blanket northwestern California. Mountains run along the Pacific coast. Inland, they flatten into the Central Valley. The peaks of the Sierra Nevada stand on the valley's eastern edge. The Mojave and other deserts cover much of eastern California. There, Death Valley dips to the lowest point in North America. It reaches 282 feet (86 meters) below sea level.

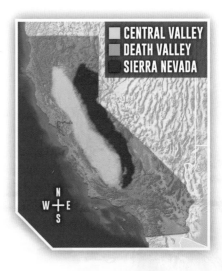

CENTRAL VALLEY
DEATH VALLEY
SIERRA NEVADA

N W E S

SIERRA NEVADA

CALIFORNIA'S FUTURE: DROUGHT AND DISASTER

High temperatures and low rainfall put California at risk of drought. Droughts can limit community water supplies and farmers' harvests. Droughts also create conditions for raging wildfires to race through dry brush and forests.

DEATH VALLEY

SEASONAL HIGHS AND LOWS

SPRING
HIGH: 69°F (21°C)
LOW: 47°F (8°C)

SUMMER
HIGH: 83°F (28°C)
LOW: 58°F (14°C)

FALL
HIGH: 73°F (23°C)
LOW: 50°F (10°C)

WINTER
HIGH: 59°F (15°C)
LOW: 40°F (4°C)

°F = degrees Fahrenheit
°C = degrees Celsius

California has warm, dry summers and cool, rainy winters. The north is cooler than the south. In the mountains, winters may bring heavy snow. Deserts are hot with little rain. Death Valley reaches some of the world's hottest temperatures!

BLACK BEAR

California is home to a wide variety of animals. Black bears search for nuts, berries, and insects in the forests. Bighorn sheep easily cross rough ground in the Sierra Nevada. They flee from mountain lions, coyotes, and other predators. Huge California condors soar through southern skies. Off the coast, sea otters dive for sea urchins in kelp forests. California sea lions climb out of the ocean to sun themselves on rocky shores.

Greater roadrunners in the Mojave Desert sprint after tarantulas, rattlesnakes, and other prey. Slow-moving desert tortoises head underground to escape the strong desert sun.

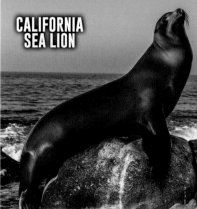
CALIFORNIA SEA LION

GREATER ROADRUNNER

BIGHORN SHEEP

DESERT TORTOISE

CALIFORNIA
CONDOR

PREHISTORIC WILDLIFE

California was once home to dire wolves, Columbian mammoths, and saber-toothed cats. They lived more than 10,000 years ago. Today, scientists unearth these animals' remains at the La Brea Tar Pits in Los Angeles.

CALIFORNIA CONDOR

Life Span: about 60 years
Status: critically endangered

California condor range =

LEAST CONCERN	NEAR THREATENED	VULNERABLE	ENDANGERED	CRITICALLY ENDANGERED	EXTINCT IN THE WILD	EXTINCT

PEOPLE AND COMMUNITIES

Almost 40 million people call California home. It has more people than any other state! California's population is mostly **urban**. More than three out of every four Californians live around San Diego, Los Angeles, and San Francisco.

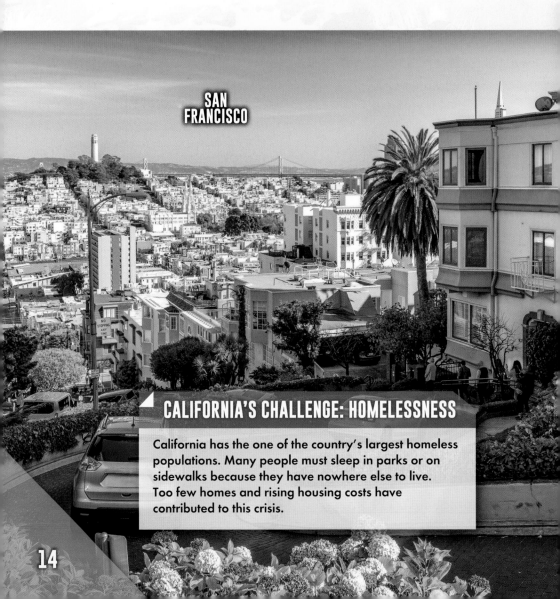

SAN FRANCISCO

CALIFORNIA'S CHALLENGE: HOMELESSNESS

California has the one of the country's largest homeless populations. Many people must sleep in parks or on sidewalks because they have nowhere else to live. Too few homes and rising housing costs have contributed to this crisis.

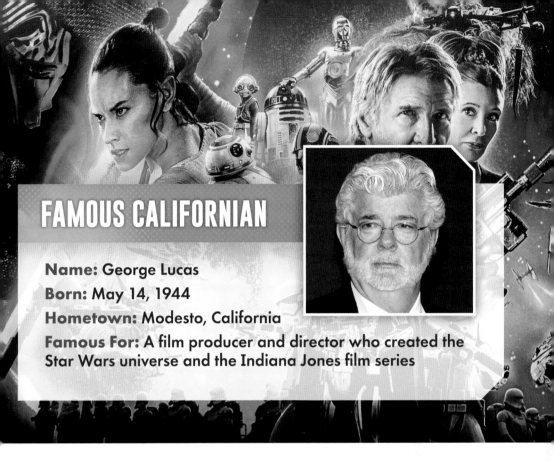

FAMOUS CALIFORNIAN

Name: George Lucas
Born: May 14, 1944
Hometown: Modesto, California
Famous For: A film producer and director who created the Star Wars universe and the Indiana Jones film series

California is a **diverse** state. Hispanic people make up the largest **ethnic** group. Californians with **ancestors** from Europe are the next-largest group. Other major groups include Asian Americans and African Americans or Black people. California's Native

American population is the country's largest. Many belong to the Yurok, Chumash, or Pomo tribes. About one in four Californians are **immigrants**. Most have arrived from Mexico, the Philippines, Vietnam, India, and China.

San Diego is California's second-largest city. It sits on the Pacific Ocean and borders Mexico. The city is called the Birthplace of California. Junípero Serra founded it in 1769 as the first mission. Early on, San Diego's biggest industries were fishing and farming.

Today, the city is a major port with a large U.S. Navy base. San Diego's warm weather and beaches draw thousands of visitors. The city's **culture** comes alive at Balboa Park. This sprawling park boasts gardens, hiking trails, and theaters. It offers 17 science, art, and history museums. The park is also home to the famous San Diego Zoo!

BALBOA PARK

DISNEYLAND

Disneyland opened in 1955. Its rides and shows feature Disney characters and films, from Mickey Mouse to *Star Wars*. Disneyland draws about 19 million tourists every year!

Agriculture is among California's most important industries. Farmers in the Central Valley grow 250 types of crops. These include grapes, rice, nuts, and berries. California's farmers produce food for much of the country. **Tourism** is a key **service industry**. Many workers have jobs at theme parks, restaurants, and hotels. In Los Angeles, many Californians work in film and television. The city is the center of the country's entertainment industry.

The San Francisco area hosts a booming technology industry. Nearby **Silicon Valley** is home to Facebook, Google, and Apple. **Manufacturing** also employs many Californians. Factory workers produce electronics, **aerospace** materials, and chemicals.

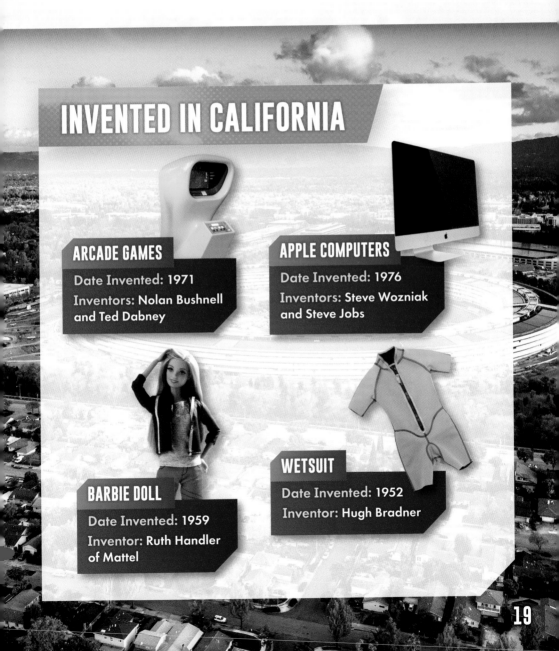

INVENTED IN CALIFORNIA

ARCADE GAMES
Date Invented: 1971

Inventors: Nolan Bushnell and Ted Dabney

APPLE COMPUTERS
Date Invented: 1976

Inventors: Steve Wozniak and Steve Jobs

BARBIE DOLL
Date Invented: 1959

Inventor: Ruth Handler of Mattel

WETSUIT
Date Invented: 1952

Inventor: Hugh Bradner

CALIFORNIA ROLLS

A FAST-FOOD FIRST

The first McDonald's restaurant opened in San Bernardino in 1940. It was called McDonald's Bar-B-Q. Today, about 36,000 locations operate in more than 100 countries!

California's food is as diverse as its population. Tacos and other Mexican foods are popular everywhere. San Diego introduced the California burrito with **carne asada**. Salsa, avocado, cheese, and french fries also fill the burrito. San Francisco diners dig into *cioppino*. This Italian seafood stew is served with the city's famous sourdough bread. Los Angeles is known for its take on Japanese sushi. Its California rolls are made with avocado, cucumber, and crab.

Many Californians shop at **farmers markets**. They buy avocados, artichokes, and other produce. They turn these into simple but flavorful dishes such as guacamole or Hollywood's classic Cobb salad.

CIOPPINO

GUACAMOLE

4 SERVINGS

Have an adult help you make this favorite dip!

INGREDIENTS

2 ripe avocados
1 Roma tomato
1/4 red onion
1 garlic clove

1 jalapeño
1 lime
10 cilantro stems
1/4 teaspoon salt

DIRECTIONS

1. Cut the avocados in half and remove the pits from the centers.

2. Use a spoon to scoop the avocado into a bowl.

3. Dice the tomato and onion. Mince the garlic.

4. Cut the jalapeño in half. Carefully remove the seeds if you do not like spicy foods. Then, mince the jalapeño.

5. Remove the cilantro leaves from the stems. Roughly chop the leaves.

6. Add the tomato, onion, garlic, jalapeño, cilantro, and salt to the avocados. Use a fork to mash them all together.

7. Cut the lime in half. Squeeze juice into the mashed avocado mixture.

8. Enjoy on toast or with tortilla chips!

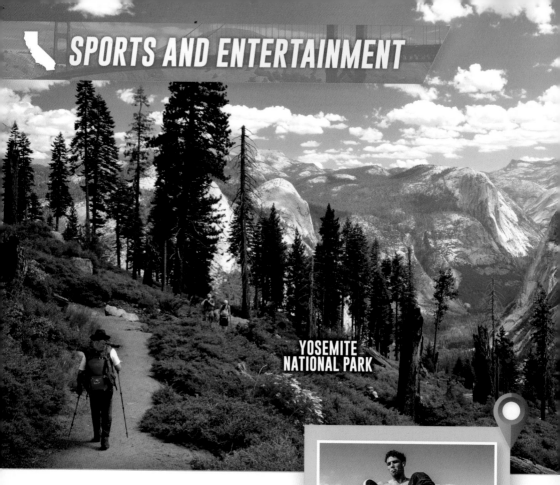

YOSEMITE
NATIONAL PARK

THE BIRTH OF SKATEBOARDING

California surfers invented skateboarding in the 1950s. They combined wooden boards and wheels from roller skates to make the first skateboards.

California is a great place for outdoor lovers. The state has nine national parks where people hike and camp in the wilderness. Yosemite is one of the country's most popular parks. There, visitors walk among the giant sequoia trees. Snowy mountains are popular spots for skiers and snowboarders. Surfers ride ocean waves off the coast. On land, people do tricks on skateboards.

Hollywood Bowl in Los Angeles is one of many outdoor **amphitheaters**. Californians can watch rock concerts and symphonies under the sky. Professional sports are also popular. Californians cheer for baseball, basketball, football, hockey, and soccer teams!

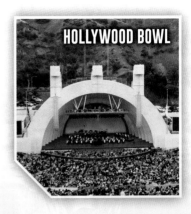

HOLLYWOOD BOWL

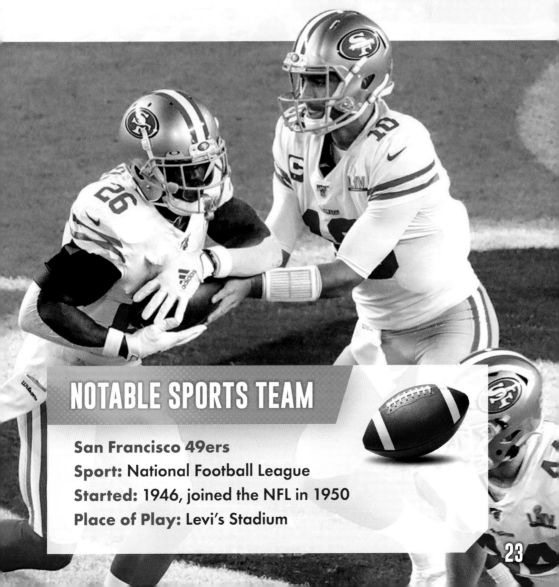

NOTABLE SPORTS TEAM

San Francisco 49ers
Sport: National Football League
Started: 1946, joined the NFL in 1950
Place of Play: Levi's Stadium

FESTIVALS AND TRADITIONS

CHINESE GOLDEN DRAGON PARADE

Each New Year's Day, Pasadena hosts the Tournament of Roses. It kicks off with a parade featuring flower-covered floats. Then two of the country's best college football teams take the field at the Rose Bowl. Late January or February brings the Lunar New Year. The Asian-American community in Los Angeles celebrates with the Chinese Golden Dragon Parade and Festival. In July, fans of comic books and video games attend the popular San Diego Comic-Con.

June brings as many as one million people together for the colorful San Francisco Pride Parade and Celebration. This lively festival gives everyone the chance to celebrate love and being themselves!

GARLIC CAPITAL OF THE WORLD

Gilroy is known as the Garlic Capital of the World. In July, its Gilroy Garlic Festival features live music, cooking contests, and a lot of food. Visitors can even try garlic ice cream!

SAN FRANCISCO PRIDE

1542
As many as 300,000 Native Americans live in California when the first Europeans arrive

1821
Mexico wins control of California from Spain

1848
The California Gold Rush begins with the discovery of gold at Sutter's Mill

1834
The Mexican government ends the missions

1769
Junípero Serra founds California's first Spanish mission, San Diego

1850
California becomes the 31st state

1923

**Walt Disney
Animation Studios opens**

2013

**Pinnacles National Park
becomes California's ninth
national park**

1937

The Golden Gate Bridge opens

2018

**The Camp Fire is the deadliest
and most destructive wildfire in
California history**

CALIFORNIA FACTS

Nicknames: The Golden State

Motto: *Eureka* (I have found it)

Date of Statehood: September 9, 1850 (the 31st state)

Capital City: Sacramento ★

Other Major Cities: San Francisco, Los Angeles, San Diego

Area: 163,695 square miles (423,968 square kilometers); California is the third-largest state.

Population

39,538,223
(2020)

STATE FLAG

CALIFORNIA REPUBLIC

Adopted in 1911, California's flag features the state animal, the grizzly bear. It stands for strength. The words *California Republic* appear beneath the bear. A red star represents the state's independence. The flag's white background is a symbol for California's purity. The red stripe across the bottom represents courage.

INDUSTRY

Main Exports

JOBS

MANUFACTURING
6%

FARMING AND NATURAL RESOURCES
2%

GOVERNMENT
12%

SERVICES
80%

computers

electronics

transportation equipment

crops

Natural Resources
timber, soil, natural gas, oil, water

GOVERNMENT

Federal Government

52 REPRESENTATIVES | **2** SENATORS

54 ELECTORAL VOTES

USA

CA

State Government

80 REPRESENTATIVES | **40** SENATORS

STATE SYMBOLS

STATE BIRD
CALIFORNIA QUAIL

STATE ANIMAL
CALIFORNIA GRIZZLY BEAR

STATE FLOWER
CALIFORNIA POPPY

STATE TREE
CALIFORNIA REDWOOD

GLOSSARY

aerospace—related to designing and building spacecraft

agriculture—the practice of raising crops and animals

amphitheaters—round, outdoor theaters with many levels of seats

ancestors—relatives who lived long ago

carne asada—grilled strips of spicy beef that are commonly used in Mexican cooking

convert—to change a person's religion

culture—the beliefs, arts, and ways of life in a place or society

diverse—made up of people or things that are different from one another

ethnic—related to a group of people who share customs and an identity

farmers markets—markets where local farmers sell goods

immigrants—people who move to a new country

manufacturing—a field of work in which people use machines to make products

missions—places where people live while spreading a religious faith

observatory—a building that is used for studying the sky, stars, or weather

service industry—a group of businesses that perform tasks for people or other businesses

Silicon Valley—a region of western California where many high-tech companies are based

tourism—the business of people traveling to visit other places

traditional—related to customs, ideas, or beliefs handed down from one generation to the next

urban—related to cities and city life

AT THE LIBRARY

Blashfield, Jean F. *The California Gold Rush and the '49ers*. North Mankato, Minn.: Capstone Press, 2018.

Hamilton, S. L. *Fleeing California Wildfires*. Minneapolis, Minn.: Abdo Publishing, 2020.

Smith-Llera, Danielle. *The Chumash: The Past and Present of California's Seashell People*. North Mankato, Minn.: Capstone Press, 2017.

ON THE WEB

FACTSURFER

Factsurfer.com gives you a safe, fun way to find more information.

1. Go to www.factsurfer.com.

2. Enter "California" into the search box and click 🔍.

3. Select your book cover to see a list of related content.

arts, 17, 23

capital (see Sacramento)

challenge, 14

Chinese Golden Dragon Parade and Festival, 24

climate, 11, 17

Death Valley, 10, 11

Disneyland, 18

fast facts, 28–29

festivals, 24–25

food, 20–21, 25

future, 11

Gilroy Garlic Festival, 25

Griffith Park, 4–5

history, 5, 8–9, 13, 16, 18, 20, 22

Hollywood, 5, 21

inventions, 19

landmarks, 4, 5, 9, 13, 17, 18, 22, 23

landscape, 4, 5, 6, 7, 10–11, 12, 18, 22

location, 6–7

Los Angeles, 4, 6, 7, 13, 14, 18, 20, 23, 24

Lucas, George, 15

McDonald's, 20

Mojave Desert, 10, 12

outdoor activities, 17, 22, 23

Pacific Ocean, 4, 5, 6, 7, 10, 16

people, 8, 9, 14–15, 24

recipe, 21

Sacramento, 6, 7

San Diego, 6, 7, 8, 14, 16–17, 20, 24

San Diego Comic-Con, 24

San Francisco, 6, 7, 8, 14, 19, 20, 25

San Francisco 49ers, 23

San Francisco Pride Parade and Celebration, 25

Serra, Junípero, 16

Sierra Nevada, 10, 12

size, 6

sports, 22, 23, 24

timeline, 26–27

Tournament of Roses, 24

wildlife, 12–13

working, 5, 11, 16, 17, 18–19